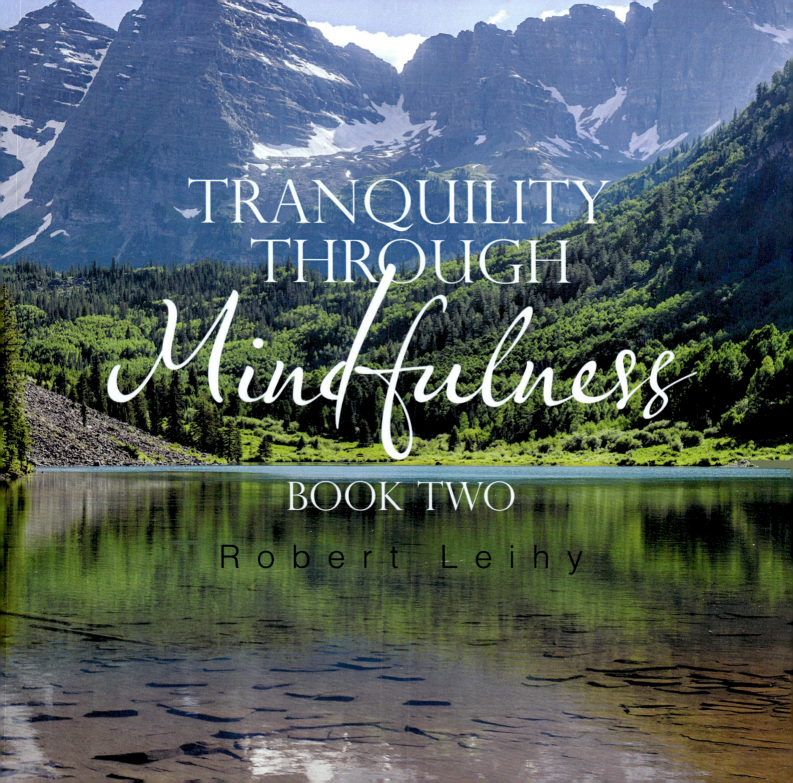

TRANQUILITY THROUGH *Mindfulness*

BOOK TWO

Robert Leihy

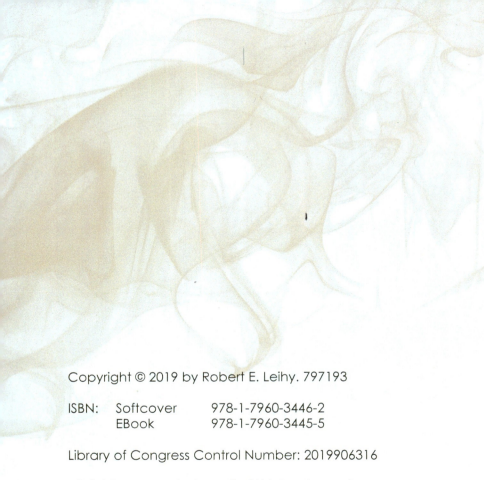

To order additional copies of this book, contact:
Xlibris
1-888-795-4274
www.Xlibris.com
Orders@Xlibris.com

TRANQUILITY
THROUGH
Mindfulness

BOOK TWO

Relaxation

AFTER A SUCCESSFUL SPA TREATMENT, A PERSON COULD BE LEFT IN NEAR-PERFECT RELAXATION. A RELAXED PERSON WOULD FEEL CONTENTED PHYSICALLY AND WOULD BE MENTALLY AT PEACE WITH THE WORLD AND WITH HIMSELF. HE WOULD BE SATISFIED IN THE HERE-AND-NOW. HE WOULD FEEL NO NEEDS OR DESIRES. AT THE SAME TIME, HE WOULD CONTINUE TO PERCEIVE THE WORLD WITH RELAXED ALERTNESS AND NORMAL MENTAL ACUITY. STRESSES WOULD SEEM TO BE AT A DISTANCE. MUSCLE TENSIONS WOULD BE REPLACED WITH LUXURIOUS AND RADIANT FEELINGS IN THE SKIN CAUSED BY BLISS HORMONES. HE WOULD BE ABLE TO MOVE ABOUT IN A "BUBBLE" OF PEACE. THIS IDEAL OF THIS STATE OF BEING COULD ALSO BE CALLED THE "MINDFUL" STATE OR THE "ENLIGHTENED" STATE.

THE MINDFULNESS PHILOSOPHY AND OTHERS POINT OUT THAT THIS SAME STATE OF BEING CAN ALSO BE APPROACHED AND EVEN REACHED NATURALLY WITH PRACTICE ALONE. ALSO, IT CAN BE QUITE INDEPENDENT OF CURRENT OUTSIDE CIRCUMSTANCES. IT CAN BRING GREATER TRANQUILITY TO DAILY LIFE.

SINCE OUR EXISTENCE PRESENTS US WITH A COMPLEX NETWORK OF POSITIVES AND NEGATIVES, AN APPROPRIATE GLOBAL WORLDVIEW, DISCUSSED LATER, WOULD BE NECESSARY TO MAINTAIN THE MINDFUL PERSPECTIVE DAY BY DAY. ANY KIND OF MENTAL FRETTING WOULD INTERFERE WITH IT.

THE SEARCH FOR WELL-BEING IS PART OF THE SURVIVAL INSTINCT, SO BY ITSELF IT INCURS NO GUILT.

SINCE STRESS IS FELT AND EXPRESSED EXCLUSIVELY IN MUSCLE TENSIONS, INCREASED RELAXATION REDUCES IT. SUCH RELAXATION CAN BE A REFUGE FROM STRESS AND FOR THIS REASON ALONE IS WORTH PRACTICING. UNLIKE SOME OTHER FORMS OF DIVERSION OR ESCAPE, IT IS ENTIRELY SAFE, SATISFYING, HEALTHY, ALWAYS AVAILABLE, LEGAL, AND COST FREE.

DEEP RELAXATION DOES NOT NEGATIVELY AFFECT JUDGMENT, DEXTERITY, OR ALERTNESS. TASKS REQUIRING CAREFUL AND PATIENT CONTROL ARE BEST DONE WHILE RELAXED. NO ONE WANTS A NERVOUS SURGEON.

PERHAPS SOME PEOPLE WHO DEPEND ON A LESS HEALTHY FORM OF DIVERSION COULD GRADUALLY ADD AND SUBSTITUTE DEEP RELAXATION FOR IT..

THE MINDFULNESS PHILOSOPHY POINTS OUT THAT IT IS POSSIBLE TO LEARN AND TO PRACTICE A RELAXATION AND "LETTING GO" RESPONSE TO THREATS IN GENERAL. IT IS AN APPLICATION OF THE SYSTEMATIC DESENSITIZATION TECHNIQUE TO THREATS IN GENERAL RATHER THAN TO JUST ONE IN PARTICULAR. AN INSTINCTIVE FIGHT-OR-FLIGHT IMPULSE CAN BE QUICKLY SUBDUED WITH A RELAXATION RESPONSE. A BRIEF MOMENT MIGHT BE NEEDED TO EVALUATE THE TRUE SEVERITY OF THE THREAT BEFORE THE RELEASE OF THE RELAXATION RESPONSE. ONE CAN INSTANTLY "KEEP HIS COOL" IN MOST LESS-THAN-LIFE-THREATENING SITUATIONS.

AS RELAXATION BECOMES A MORE HABITUAL AUTOMATIC RESPONSE, ONE STAYS MORE TRANQUIL DURING THE UPS AND DOWNS OF THE DAY WITHOUT EVEN THINKING ABOUT IT. THE MIND STILL PERCEIVES ANY STRESS OR THREATS, BUT RELAXATION BECOMES THE ALMOST IMMEDIATE CONDITIONED RESPONSE.

RELAXATION PRACTICE IS THE ROYAL ROAD TO CONTENTMENT. IT IS A SINGLE OBSERVABLE PATH. ONE CAN FEEL IT AND CHANGE HIS POSITION ON IT.

OTHER PHILOSOPHIES AND RELIGIONS THAT PROPOSE THE SAME SORTS OF EXPERIENCES ARE CONCEPTUALLY MORE SWEEPING AND DETAILED IN NATURE THAN IS THE SINGLE PATH OF RELAXATION.

NEGATIVES CAN STILL BE THOUGHT ABOUT AND ANALYZED WHEN RELAXED, BUT THE NEGATIVE EMOTIONAL COMPONENT IS REDUCED OR NOT PRESENT AT ALL. CONSTRUCTIVE ANALYSIS OF NEGATIVES WHILE RELAXED CAN HELP TO REACH SATISFYING AND OBJECTIVE CONCLUSIONS.

TO PRACTICE RELAXATION, ONE CAN SIMPLY LET GO OF MUSCLE TENSION A LITTLE MORE AT THE END OF EACH EXHALATION. SOFT BREATHING HELPS BECAUSE THE BREATHING MUSCLES ARE VERY SENSITIVE TO BOTH MENTAL AND PHYSICAL STRESS. RESTING THE AWARENESS ON NEWLY RELAXED MUSCLES IS OF BENEFIT BECAUSE THE MEMORY OF THE SENSATION BY ITSELF CAN HELP TO EVOKE THE SAME EXPERIENCE LATER.

THE VOLUNTARY MUSCLE TENSION THAT IS USED TO MOVE THE BODY ABOUT IS NOT A PROBLEM BECAUSE IT CAN BE RELAXED INSTANTLY AT WILL. IT IS THE CHRONIC INVOLUNTARY TENSIONS ASSOCIATED WITH STRESS THAT CAUSE DISCONTENT. WHEN THESE HAVE BEEN SUBDUED, IT IS POSSIBLE TO MOVE THROUGH THE DAY IN A RELAXED, CONTENTED FASHION USING JUST THE VOLUNTARY MUSCLES.

THE AUTHOR SUSPECTS THAT CHRONIC TENSION IN THE INTERCOSTAL BREATHING MUSCLES CAN EVENTUALLY CAUSE CHEST PAINS AND VARIOUS PHYSICAL PROBLEMS INSIDE THE RIB CAGE DUE TO CHRONIC INTERNAL PRESSURE THERE. HE STRONGLY SUSPECTS THAT PRACTICING HIS RELEASE OF THIS TENSION GRADUALLY CURED HIS ATRIAL FIBRILLATION (PALPITATIONS OF THE HEART) YEARS AGO. THERE CERTAINLY SEEMED TO BE A TIME CORRELATION AS WELL AS A PHYSICAL FEELING CORRELATION BETWEEN THE TWO. HE BELIEVES THAT RESEARCH IS WARRANTED IN THIS AREA.

ONE CANNOT STRIVE F0F RELAXATION BECAUSE STRIVING IS TENSION. IT IS THE SKILL OF LETTING GO OF MUSCLE TENSION THAT FACILITATES PROGRESS. SELF-CRITICISM FOR LACK OF DESIRED PROGRESS CAN BE ANOTHER TENSION THAT NEEDS TO BE RELAXED. ONE CAN PRACTICE BEING CONTENT WHERE HE IS.

PRACTICE IN LETTING GO IS THE TRAINING OF INVOLUNTARY MUSCLE TENSIONS TO BECOME VOLUNTARY. THIS MAKES THEM RESPONSIVE TO THE WILL.

OFTENTIMES MOVING ON TO ANOTHER MENTAL TOPIC OR ANOTHER PHYSICAL SITUATION CAN BE AN ESCAPE FROM TENSION.

RELAXATION PRACTICE IS A PLEASURE THAT CAN BE DONE AT ANYTIME. EVEN THOUGH IT IS VERY SIMPLE, IT CAN LEAD TO PROFOUND AND LASTING IMPROVEMENTS IN GENERAL WELL-BEING AND OUTLOOK.

A HABITUAL ATTITUDE OF LETTING GO OF TENSION AND REMAINING IN THE CURRENT RELAXED STATE IS USEFUL. HABIT CAN OVERRIDE FIGHT-OR-FLIGHT IMPULSES.

Global Worldview

A GLOBAL WORLDVIEW IS A CONCEPT LIKE ANY OTHER CONCEPT, BUT IT CAN BE ASSOCIATED WITH ANYTHING AND EVERYTHING IN ONE'S EXISTENCE. THE CONCEPT THAT LIFE IS GOOD IS A GLOBAL WORLDVIEW.

A POSITIVE AND VALID WORLDVIEW THAT ACCOMMODATES ALL WORLDLY CIRCUMSTANCES WOULD BE NECESSARY IN ORDER TO MAINTAIN A PERFECT MINDFUL OUTLOOK AND STATE OF BEING. THIS INCLUDES ACCEPTANCE OF THE NEGATIVE AND THE ABSURD. IT NEEDS TO BE A NON-JUDGMENTAL AND ACCEPTING ATTITUDE TOWARD THE FLOW OF REALITY.

AN APPROPRIATE, VALID, AND POPULAR WORLDVIEW THAT COVERS EVERYTHING STARTS WITH THE FACT THAT THE PHYSICAL UNIVERSE IS MADE ENTIRELY OF ATOMS.

WITHOUT AN ORGANIZING PRINCIPLE IN EFFECT, THE ATOMS WOULD BE SCATTERED RANDOMLY. INSTEAD, THEY ARE HIGHLY ORGANIZED INTO STRUCTURES SUCH AS THE HUMAN BODY, THE HUMAN BRAIN, THE TABLES AND THE CHAIRS, AND EVEN THE AIR THAT WE BREATHE. WE CAN SAW WOOD AND MAKE TABLES, BUT WE CANNOT COLLECT ATOMS, ORGANIZE THEM, AND MAKE THE WOOD ITSELF. OUR EXISTENCE IS COMPOSED ENTIRELY OF STRUCTURES MADE OF ORGANIZED ATOMS.

A MYSTERIOUS UNSEEN HIGHER POWER CONTINUOUSLY PLACES, MOVES, AND ORGANIZES ALL OF THE ATOMS AT ONCE TO PRODUCE OUR EVER-CHANGING EXISTENCE AS WE KNOW IT.

IF WE LOOK AT A CITY BLOCK OR A FOREST, WE KNOW FOR SURE WE DID NOT COLLECT OR ORGANIZE THE ATOMS TO CREATE EITHER OF THEM OR TO KEEP THEM RUNNING; SOMETHING ELSE IS AT WORK. WE LIVE IN A SEA OF ATOMS THAT ARE ALL SOMEHOW BEING ORGANIZED INTO THE STRUCTURES THAT MAKE UP OUR EXISTENCE.

IF THE HIGHER POWER DID NOT ORGANIZE <u>ALL</u> OF THE ATOMS, THERE WOULD BE "HOLES" FOUND IN EXISTENCE OCCUPIED BY NOTHING BUT RANDOM ATOMS. THIS IS NOT THE CASE.

Robert E. Leihy

THE HIGHER POWER MUST ORGANIZE THE ATOMS OF OUR BRAINS IN SUCH A WAY AS TO CONTINUALLY PRODUCE ALL OF OUR MINDS AND OUR CONTENTS OF CONSCIOUSNESS. IN EFFECT, THE COSMIC MOVER OF THE BRAIN ATOMS CREATES OUR MINDS, WHICH IS ACTUALLY WHERE WE LIVE EXCLUSIVELY. OUR MINDS INCLUDE OUR AWARENESS, OUR THOUGHTS, OUR CONCEPTS, AND OUR SENSE OF SELF. IT ALSO INCLUDES THE PERSPECTIVE OF A FREE WILL AND A COHERENT RELATIONSHIP BETWEEN THE SELF AND THE APPARENT EVERYDAY WORLD WHICH IS ALSO MADE OF ATOMS. THE MIND-BRAIN BOUNDARY IS CERTAINLY A MYSTERY, AND IT CERTAINLY TRANSLATES CONSIDERABLE DATA.

THE DALAI LAMA REFERRED TO THE MYSTERY OF THE SOURCE OF THOUGHT WHEN HE ASKED

THE QUESTION: "HOW DOES THE BRAIN KNOW WHAT THOUGHT TO THINK NEXT?".

A LOGICAL CONCLUSION TO THIS LINE OF REASONING WOULD BE THAT THE HIGHER POWER, THE ORGANIZER OF THE ATOMS, CREATES <u>ALL</u> OF THE ELEMENTS OF EXISTENCE, EVEN OUR THOUGHTS. "ALL THE WORLD IS A STAGE AND THE PEOPLE ARE PLAYERS WITH AWARENESS".

THE HIGHER POWER ALSO DIRECTS COUNTLESS MENTAL AND PHYSICAL DRAMAS ALL AROUND THE WORLD ALL DAY LONG. BESIDES BEING ALL-PERVADING, ALL-SEEING, ALL-KNOWING, AND ALL-POWERFUL, HE KNOWS AND MANIPULATES ALL DRAMA. IT IS DIFFICULT TO CONCEPTUALIZE A BEING WITH SUCH CAPABILITIES, BUT IT MUST EXIST OTHERWISE WE WOULD NOT BE HERE.

THE HUMAN DRAMA IS THE MOST COMPLEX ORGANIZATION OF ATOMS IN THE KNOWN UNIVERSE. AS SUCH, IT COULD BE ASSUMED TO BE ITS HIGHEST KNOWN PURPOSE.

DRAMA REQUIRES BOTH THE POSITIVES AND THE NEGATIVES. THIS MIGHT BE AN EXPLANATION FOR THE NEGATIVES IN EXISTENCE. PERHAPS IT IS THE INTERACTION BETWEEN THE POSITIVES AND THE NEGATIVES THAT SOMEHOW ALLOWS SELF-AWARENESS TO EXIST IN A UNIVERSE OF MINDLESS ATOMS.

PHRASES IN OUR LANGUAGE CONFIRM OUR GENERAL ACCEPTANCE OF THE RELIGIOUS POINT OF VIEW. FOR EXAMPLE, IT WAS GOD'S WILL, THANK GOD IT HAPPENED, GOD WILLING IT WILL HAPPEN, SWEAR TO GOD, THE LORD MOVES IN MYSTERIOUS WAYS, ONLY GOD KNOWS, WHAT WILL BE WILL BE, THERE BUT FOR THE GRACE OF GOD GO I. OH, MY GOD.

THE FIRST SUNLIGHT IN WASHINGTON D.C. FALLS ON A PLAQUE ATOP THE WASHINGTON MONUMENT THAT SAYS "PRAISE GOD".

EXISTENCE IS ENTIRELY COHERENT AND CONSISTENT. THERE ARE NO HOLES, OVERLAPS, OR TIME. DIMENSION, OR DRAMA DISTORTIONS TO BE FOUND IN IT. IT RUNS LIKE A FINE WATCH. NATURAL LAWS PRECISELY LIMIT IT AND CONSTRAIN ITS EXPRESSION AND ARE SEEMINGLY ENTIRELY RELIABLE.

IT IS POSSIBLE TO DEFINE ONESELF AS A STAND-ALONE ATOMIC PROCESS EXISTING WITHIN THE LARGER ATOMIC PROCESS THAT MAKES UP HIS SURROUNDINGS. ONE'S SKIN BECOMES THE BOUNDARY BETWEEN THE SELF AND THE REST OF EXISTENCE.

ON THE OTHER HAND, ONE CAN DEFINE HIMSELF AS AN ATOMIC PROCESS COMPLETELY BLENDED IN WITH AND FLOWING ALONG WITH THE SURROUNDING OVERALL ATOMIC PROCESS. HIS SKIN BECOMES A LAYER OF ATOMS THAT INEXTRICABLY JOINS HIM WITH THE REST OF THE ATOMS OF EXISTENCE. THE DROP OF WATER BECOMES THE OCEAN. EACH POINT IF VIEW HAS MANY IMPLICATIONS, AND BOTH ARE VALID. WE REALLY DO LIVE ENTIRELY IN OUR MINDS AND WE RELATE TO THEIR CONTENTS AS REALITIES. AT THE SAME TIME, ATOMS SEEM TO BE A REALITY AND THEY HAVE TO BE ORGANIZED SOMEHOW TO PRODUCE THE PHYSICAL STRUCTURES AND THE MENTAL EXPERIENCES THAT MAKE UP OUR EXISTENCE.

IN ANY CASE, OUR STREAM OF MENTAL CONSCIOUS IS OUR ONLY EXISTENCE AND IT IS ALL THAT WE HAVE.

EXISTENCE, INCLUDING OURSELVES, CAN BE CONCEPTUALIZED AS MIRACULOUSLY EMERGING FROM AN UNKNOWN SOURCE AND CHANGING SEEMINGLY BY ITSELF MOMENT BY MOMENT. WHY IT TAKES THE PARTICULAR ATOMIC FORM THAT IT DOES, ONLY GOD KNOWS. WHY THE NEGATIVES ARE ADDED TO IT IS UNKNOWN, BUT APPARENTLY WE ARE OBLIGED TO ACCEPT THEM, TO ENDURE THEM, AND TO TRY TO REDUCE THEM BOTH FOR OURSELVES AND OTHERS.

OUR PERSONAL EGOS HAVE BEEN DESIGNED BY OUR BRAINS IN SUCH A WAY THAT IT SEEMS TO US THAT WE HAVE THE FREE WILL TO CHOOSE OUR ACTIONS AND OUR THOUGHTS. WE CAN CHOOSE HOW WE AFFECT THE WORLD. WE CAN CHOOSE THE CONCEPTS THAT WE WISH TO USE TO LIVE BY. SINCE OUR EGOS HAVE BEEN ENDOWED WITH THESE ABILITIES, IT SEEMS THAT WE ARE INTENDED TO USE THEM.

ONE CAN CHOOSE TO LEARN, DEEPEN, AND PRACTICE THE OVERALL MINDFUL PERSPECTIVE OF THE WORLD. IT WOULD INCLUDE PLEASURABLE DEEP RELAXATION, ACCEPTANCE OF CURRENT CIRCUMSTANCES, ATTENTIVENESS AND SUFFICIENT DETACHMENT FROM THE LESS USEFUL DRAMAS THAT TEND TO UNFOLD IN HIS EXISTENCE. THE SKILL OF "LETTING GO" CAN BE APPLIED TO THE FLOW OF CIRCUMSTANCES AS WELL AS TO MUSCLE TENSIONS. ONE CAN "GO WITH THE FLOW" AND "LET THE WORLD GO BY" WITH MINIMAL RESISTANCE. AS DANCERS SOMETIME SAY: "LET THE BODY DANCE ITSELF".

EVEN THOUGH EMERGING EXISTENCE IS A MYSTERY, ONE CAN BE ACCEPTING OF AND CONTENTED WITHIN IT AND STILL MAKE ANY ASSUMPTIONS HE WISHES REGARDING ITS NATURE AND PURPOSE. SEEKING AND FINDING APPROPRIATE AND AUTHENTIC STRUCTURE FOR ONE'S EXISTENCE SEEMS TO BE A NATURAL HUMAN TENDENCY. NEVERTHELESS, THE BROADEST STRUCTURE OF ALL WILL STILL BE THAT'LL OF EXISTENCE IS A MYSTERY.

IF ONE'S CONCEPT OF BEING A PART OF EVERYTHING COMES TO BE MORE VIVID AND AUTHENTIC, CONCERN ABOUT THE FUTURE DIMINISHES. THE CONCEPT THAT A MERCIFUL GOD AND FATE WILL PREVAIL STARTS TO TAKE ITS PLACE. IT IS A BIG STEP TOWARD DEEPER TRANQUILITY AND A REDUCTION OF FEELINGS OF ALIENATION TO TRUST A HIGHER POWER. IT IS ALSO A REDUCES THE FIGHT-OR FLIGHT INSTINCTS AS WELL AS ANY CHRONIC RESENTMENT OF THE NEGATIVES.

THE CONCEPT THAT GOD CAN BE TRUSTED TO ULTIMATELY BE MERCIFUL CAN BE A REFUGE IN A TUMULTUOUS WORLD. BOTH FAITH AND ANXIETY ARE MENTAL PICTURES OF A HYPOTHETICAL FUTURE. FAITH IS THE CLOSER ONE TO TRANQUILITY.

PAYING RESPECT TO THE MIRACLE OF EXISTENCE AND TO ITS CREATOR CAN BE A FORM OF A PERSONAL EXPRESSION OF GRATITUDE FOR THE PRIVILEGE OF BEING HERE AS A PART OF THIS UNFOLDING MYSTERY.

Daily Tranquility

A VIRTUOUS LIFESTYLE IS THE KEY TO A CONTINUOUS TRANQUIL AND GRATIFYING DAILY EXISTENCE.

HAVING THE INTENTION AND HABIT OF MAKING POSITIVE CONTRIBUTIONS INTO ONE'S WORLD WHEN OPPORTUNITIES ARISE WILL HELP TO INSURE A GOOD OVERALL RELATIONSHIP WITH IT. FOR INSTANCE, TREATING A PERSON WELL WILL PROBABLY LEAD ONE TO EXPECT A SIMILAR RESPONSE FROM HIM IN THE FUTURE. CARE OF ONE'S BELONGINGS AND OTHER SURROUNDINGS WILL EXTEND THEIR VALUE. IF ONE'S ENTIRE OUTSIDE WORLD IS CONCEPTUALIZED AS A SINGLE ENTITY, POSITIVE CONTRIBUTIONS TO IT WILL HELP. ONE CAN RELAX BETTER WITH THE FEELING THAT GOD AND FATE WILL LIKELY BE MERCIFUL. IT WILL

HELP ONE TO FEEL JUSTIFIED IN HIS BEING HERE. IT WILL HELP TO CREATE AND MAINTAIN A MORE POSITIVE SELF-IMAGE. IT WILL HELP ONE EXPERIENCE THE CONCEPT OF "HAVING TRUST IN GOD". IT WILL ALSO AVOID THE ACCUMULATION OF PERSONAL GUILT AND ITS ACCOMPANYING GENERAL FEELING THAT THERE ARE "VENDETTAS" OUT THERE IN THE WORLD WAITING FOR THE RIGHT MOMENT TO SPRING.

AN ABUSIVE LIFESTYLE BRINGS ABOUT FEELINGS OF DEFENSIVENESS AND GUILT. THE WORLD IN GENERAL COMES TO LOOK RETALIATORY AND HOSTILE.

THE WAY THE MIND WORKS, IT SEEMS THAT THE <u>QUALITY</u> OF ONE'S CONTRIBUTION TO HIS OUTSIDE WORLD SEEMS TO PERSIST OUT THERE AND IS EXPECTED TO EVENTUALLY COME BACK IN ONE FORM OR ANOTHER. ''AS YE SOW, SO SHALL YE REAP''. A LADY I KNEW ONCE SAID "I DESERVE EVERY BAD THING THAT EVER HAPPENED TO ME". THIS APPARENT GIVE-AND-TAKE RELATIONSHIP WITH ONE'S OUTSIDE WORLD MAY BE BASED ON THE PERCEPTION THAT ONE AND HIS WORLD SHARE THE ONE AND THE SAME OVERALL EXISTENCE, BE IT MADE OF ATOMS OR OF MIND OR OF SPIRIT. WE DEFINITELY LIVE ENTIRELY IN OUR ONE AND ONLY MIND AND EVERYTHING WE EXPERIENCE EXPRESSES ITSELF IN OUR STREAM OF CONSCIOUSNESS. 'THAT ART THOU''. IT IS SELF-AWARENESS THAT INCLUDES THE CONCEPT THAT ONE IS SEPARATE FROM HIS SURROUNDINGS INSTEAD OF THAT OF SHARING THE SAME OVERALL ATOMIC PROCESS.

A PERSON SLEEPS BETTER IF HE FEELS HE HAS A FRIENDLY RELATIONSHIP WITH HIS OUTSIDE WORLD AND IF HE. IS REASONABLY WELL CAUGHT UP WITH HIS OBLIGATIONS..

THE MIND IS THE ONE PLACE WHERE THE PHYSICAL UNIVERSE IS AWARE OF ITSELF, AND THIS AWARENESS IS OF A MENTAL EXPERIENCE THAT ONLY ASSUMEDLY REPRESENTS A PHYSICAL WORLD. THE REASON FOR THE PATH OF AWARENESS FROM GOD TO THE ATOMS TO THE BRAIN TO THE MIND TO MENTAL AWARENESS TO A MENTAL EGO-RELATIONSHIP WITH A MENTAL REPRESENTATION OF AN ASSUMED PHYSICAL WORLD MADE OF ATOMS IS A MYSTERY.

BEING ABLE TO COMFORTABLY ACCEPT THE CONCEPT THAT WE LIVE IN A MYSTERY HELPS WITH CONTENTMENT. CONSIDERABLE ENERGY CAN BE WASTED TRYING TO FIGURE IT OUT OR TO ENGAGE IN DEFENDING SOME PARTICULAR POINT OF VIEW.

PUTTING THINGS OFF UNTIL THE LAST MINUTE AND THEN RUSHING IN A PANIC CAN BE EXTREMELY DAMAGING TO RELAXATION PRACTICE. THE HABIT OF LEAVING A LITTLE EXTRA TIME FOR EVERYTHING, OBLIGATIONS AND TRAVEL, CAN TAKE ALL THAT AWAY AND LEAVE MORE ROOM FOR TRANQUILITY. TIME ITSELF CAN BE CONCEPTUALIZED AS AMBLING RATHER THAN URGENTLY RUSHING.

A GOOD HABIT FOR DAILY LIFE TRANQUILITY IS EXPRESSED IN THE SAYING: "DO IT NOW". A TRANQUIL WORLD REQUIRES A CERTAIN AMOUNT OF PLANNING AND ENGINEERING

INSTEAD OF SEEING EXISTENCE AS A FRUSTRATING ENDLESS FLOW OF NEEDS AND OBLIGATIONS, IT CAN BE SEEN AS A FANTASTIC MIRACLE OF DRAMA THAT IS SOMEHOW BEING PROVIDED FOR US. REVERENCE IS CLOSER TO TRANQUILITY THAN FRUSTRATION.

THE EXPERIENCE OF DEEP RELAXATION IN A CONTENTED BODY WITH A MIND AT PEACE IS ABOUT AS GOOD AS IT GETS HERE ON THIS PARTICULAR PLANE OF EXISTENCE.

Printed in the United States
By Bookmasters